STEM IN THE SUMMER OLYMPICS
THE SCIENCE BEHIND GYMNASTICS

by Jenny Fretland VanVoorst

Ideas for Parents and Teachers

Pogo Books let children practice reading informational text while introducing them to nonfiction features such as headings, labels, sidebars, maps, and diagrams, as well as a table of contents, glossary, and index.

Carefully leveled text with a strong photo match offers early fluent readers the support they need to succeed.

Before Reading

- "Walk" through the book and point out the various nonfiction features. Ask the student what purpose each feature serves.
- Look at the glossary together. Read and discuss the words.

Read the Book

- Have the child read the book independently.
- Invite him or her to list questions that arise from reading.

After Reading

- Discuss the child's questions. Talk about how he or she might find answers to those questions.
- Prompt the child to think more. Ask: Gymnasts use grips and chalk to control friction. Can you think of any other athletes that need to control friction?

Pogo Books are published by Jump!
5357 Penn Avenue South
Minneapolis, MN 55419
www.jumplibrary.com

Library of Congress Cataloging-in-Publication Data

Names: Fretland VanVoorst, Jenny, 1972- author.
Title: The science behind gymnastics / by Jenny Fretland VanVoorst.
Description: Pogo Books Edition. Minneapolis, Minnesota: Pogo Books are published by Jump!, [2020] | Series: STEM in the Summer Olympics | Includes index.
Identifiers: LCCN 2019008235 (print)
LCCN 2019010963 (ebook)
ISBN 9781641289078 (ebook)
ISBN 9781641289054 (hardcover: alk. paper)
Subjects: LCSH: Gymnastics–Juvenile literature.
Sports sciences–Juvenile literature.
Olympics–Juvenile literature.
Classification: LCC GV461.3 (ebook)
LCC GV461.3 .F74 2020 (print) | DDC 796.44–dc23
LC record available at https://lccn.loc.gov/2019008235

Editor: Susanne Bushman
Designer: Michelle Sonnek

Photo Credits: Meawpong3405/Shutterstock, cover (clipboard); ChislovaArina/Shutterstock, cover (rings); Ben Stansall/AFP/Getty, 1, 20-21; Africa Studio/Shutterstock, 3 (ball); xpixel/Shutterstock, 3 (ribbon); ioflo69/Shutterstock, 3 (clubs); SMAK_Photo/Shutterstock, 3 (hoop); PCN Photography/Alamy, 4; Lukas Schulze/picture alliance/Getty, 5, 23; A.RICARDO/Shutterstock, 6-7; Valery Sharifulin/TASS/Getty, 8; David Ramos/Getty, 9; Thomas Coex/AFP/Getty, 10-11, 12-13; The Asahi Shimbun/Getty, 14-15; Leonard Zhukovsky/Shutterstock, 16-17; Lukas Schulze/dpa picture alliance/Alamy, 18; Bob Thomas/Popperfoto/Getty, 19.

Printed in the United States of America at Corporate Graphics in North Mankato, Minnesota.

TABLE OF CONTENTS

CHAPTER 1
Flips and Physics..................4

CHAPTER 2
Flying High..................8

CHAPTER 3
A Grip on Friction..................18

ACTIVITIES & TOOLS
Try This!..................22
Glossary..................23
Index..................24
To Learn More..................24

CHAPTER 1

· ·

FLIPS AND PHYSICS

Flips. Twists. Turns!
Olympic gymnasts use
physics to win big!

hoop

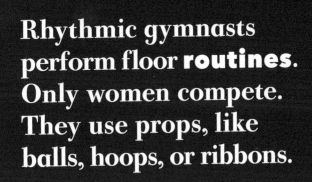

Rhythmic gymnasts perform floor **routines**. Only women compete. They use props, like balls, hoops, or ribbons.

ring

Both men and women compete in artistic gymnastics. These routines involve **apparatuses**. Like what? Rings, vaults, bars, and pommel horses.

CHAPTER 2

FLYING HIGH

It helps gymnasts to be short. Why? Their **center of gravity** is lower. The lower on the body, the easier it is to balance.

Rio2016

She sticks her landing! Bending her knees helped. How? It lowered her center of gravity even more.

Bent knees help gymnasts jump higher, too. How? They apply **force** to the ground. This is an **action force**. It is returned with a **reaction force**. It pushes the gymnasts up with more force. They fly higher into the air.

DID YOU KNOW?

Gymnastics was in the first modern Olympics in 1896. Events included rock lifting! Club swinging. Swimming was a gymnastics event in 1922.

Floor routines are done on a special floor. It is supported by springs. They increase the floor's reaction force. The gymnast bounces higher. He has more time to flip and spin. The springs also help **absorb** shock. This keeps athletes from getting hurt.

DID YOU KNOW?

Olympic gymnasts get some serious air! How high can they jump? Almost 10 feet (3 meters) high during skills!

vault

springboard

Springs help in the vault events, too. Gymnasts run toward the vault. They bounce off of a springboard. This increases the reaction force. They are launched onto the vault.

uneven
bar

Gymnastics would not be possible without **gravity**. See the uneven bars? At the top, she has **potential energy**. She swings! Gravity changes this energy. It turns to **kinetic energy**. All objects in motion have this.

TAKE A LOOK!

Bar routines require speed. How do gymnasts gain it? Take a look!

1. Kinetic energy helps the gymnast swing around the bar.

2. The gymnast bends his knees. This brings his center of gravity closer to the bar.

3. The gymnast extends his legs again. He swings around again and **dismounts**. The extra speed allows him more time in the air for skills.

③

②

①

CHAPTER 3

A GRIP ON FRICTION

Friction helps in many events. It helps gymnasts keep their grip. On what? Parallel bars. Pommel horses. Rings.

pommel horse

parallel bars

But too much friction can be a problem. Why? Friction turns into heat. When a gymnast spins, friction makes his hands hot. It might keep him from swinging freely.

Artistic gymnasts work to control friction. They powder their hands with chalk. They wear grips, too. They get the grip they need without the heat.

Olympians use physics with every move. It helps them win gold!

grip

ACTIVITIES & TOOLS

PRACTICING BALANCE

Balance is key in gymnastics. How long can you balance? Does changing your center of gravity help?

What You Need:
- a stopwatch or other timekeeping device with a seconds hand
- a friend

❶ Find a flat surface.

❷ Stand on one foot.

❸ Have your friend use a stopwatch to time you.

❹ Each time you put your foot down, have your friend stop timing. Then try again. Does your balance improve each time?

❺ Now try balancing on the other foot. Is there any difference in balance between the two feet?

❻ Try bending your knee. Does it help you balance? Try making other changes, like taking off your shoes. What helps you balance the longest?

GLOSSARY

absorb: To take in.

action force: A force applied to an object.

apparatuses: Objects on which artistic gymnastics are performed, such as vaults, bars, and balance beams.

center of gravity: The point at which weight is centered on an object and helps predict how the object will act when pulled toward Earth by gravity.

dismounts: Leaves an apparatus at the end of a routine, usually with a difficult twist or flip.

force: An action that produces, stops, or changes the shape of a movement or object.

friction: The force that slows down objects when they rub against each other.

gravity: The force that pulls objects toward the center of Earth and keeps them from floating away.

kinetic energy: The energy of motion.

physics: The science that deals with matter, energy, and their interactions.

potential energy: Stored energy that can be released to turn into kinetic energy.

reaction force: An equal force that is applied in the opposite direction of impact.

routines: Planned sets of movements.

action force 10

artistic gymnastics 7, 20

balance 8

center of gravity 8, 9, 17

chalk 20

dismounts 17

friction 18, 19, 20

gravity 16

grip 18, 20

kinetic energy 16, 17

landing 9

parallel bars 18

pommel horses 7, 18

potential energy 16

props 5

reaction force 10, 12, 15

rhythmic gymnastics 5

rings 7, 18

routines 5, 7, 12, 17

scored 7

springboard 15

springs 12, 15

uneven bars 16

vaults 7, 15

TO LEARN MORE

Finding more information is as easy as 1, 2, 3.

❶ Go to www.factsurfer.com

❷ Enter "sciencebehindgymnastics" into the search box.

❸ Choose your book to see a list of websites.

FACT SURFER